Finger Food Recipes That Are Perfect For Any Party

Lex .O Edge

Indulge in the sweetness of Raspberry Ribbons, Dipped Strawberries, and Lemon Meltaways. These elegant desserts are perfect for adding a touch of sophistication to any occasion. For a burst of flavor, try the Apricot and Orange Liqueur Parcels or the Phyllo Cups with Cappuccino Cream.

Explore unique creations like Avocado Key Lime Tartlets, Pear Chips with Cinnamon Sugar, and Billionaire's Bites. These innovative recipes offer a delightful twist on classic finger foods and are sure to be a hit with your guests.

Satisfy your chocolate cravings with Ooey Gooey Banana Bars with Cream Cheese Frosting, Caribbean Cocktail Cupcakes, and Mocha Mousse Pots. These decadent desserts are perfect for chocolate lovers and are guaranteed to leave a lasting impression.

For savory options, delight your guests with Upside-Down Mushroom Tartlets, Antipasti Pizzas, and Sun-Dried Tomato Palmiers. These savory bites are packed with flavor and are ideal for starting off your party on the right note.

Impress your guests with creative options like Chicken Liver Pate Crostini with Quince Jelly, Scallop Horseradish Finger Food, and Coconut Chicken Fingers with Banana Dip. These savory treats are perfect for satisfying appetites and are sure to be a conversation starter.

For a touch of elegance, serve Pancetta-Wrapped Figs, Dates Stuffed with Blue Cheese, and Mini Spaghetti Pies. These sophisticated options are perfect for adding a gourmet touch to your party spread.

With this book, you'll have everything you need to create a memorable and delicious spread for your next gathering. From sweet to savory, these recipes are sure to delight your guests and leave them wanting more.

Contents

Chapter I: Sweet Recipes

||||||||||||||||||||||||||||||||||||||||||||||||||||||||||||||||||||||||||||

(1)   Raspberry Ribbons

These pretty little jam-filled cookies will brighten up any party spread.

Makes: 40

Preparation Time: 45mins

Ingredient List:

Cookies:

- ½ cup white sugar
- 1 cup salted butter (room temperature)
- 1 teaspoon vanilla essence
- 1 medium egg
- ½ teaspoons baking powder

- 2¼ cups all-purpose flour
- ¼ teaspoons sea salt
- ½ cup organic raspberry jam

||||||||||||||||||||||||||||||||||||||||||||||||||||||||||||||||||||||||||||

Instructions:

1. Preheat the main oven to 350 degrees F. Line cookie sheets with aluminum foil.

2. Cream together the sugar and butter until fluffy. Beat in the vanilla and egg.

3. Sift in the baking powder, flour, and salt. Mix until incorporated.

4. Divide the dough into 4 equally-sized pieces.

5. Roll each piece of dough into a 10x2½") logs. Place the logs on the cookie sheets a few inches apart.

6. Make a ½" well down the center of each log using your fingertip.

7. Place in the oven and bake for 9-11 minutes. Take out of the oven and spoon raspberry jam into each well.

8. Return to the oven for another 12-15 minutes. Allow to cool for 2-3 minutes before placing on a chopping board and slicing into ¾" cookies.

9. Set aside to cool completely.

(2) Dipped Strawberries

Simple yet totally delicious, sweet juicy strawberries dipped in rich chocolate and covered with pistachios taste as splendid as they look.

Makes: 20

Preparation Time: 50mins

Ingredient List:

- 8 ounces semisweet choc chips
- 20 large sweet strawberries (washed, patted dry)
- ⅓ cup pistachios (finely chopped)

IIIIIIIIIIIIIIIIIIIIIIIIIIIIIIIIIIIIIIIIIIIIIIIIIIIIIIIIIIIIIIIIIIIIIII

Instructions:

1. Melt the choc chips gently using a double boiler, stirring continually.

2. Take off the heat and set aside for one moment.

3. Cover a cookie sheet with wax paper.

4. Using the stem of the strawberries, dip each in the melted chocolate. Gently twirl to drip off any excess chocolate and set on the cookie sheet. Repeat until all of the strawberries are coated.

5. Sprinkle with the pistachios.

6. Chill for 20-30 minutes, until set.

(3) Lemon Meltaways

Sweet little melt in the mouth morsels flavored with fresh lemon juice and zest. Be warned; they're addictive!

Makes: 42

Preparation Time: 45mins

Ingredient List:

- ¾ cup + 2tbsp salted butter (room temperature)
- 1½ cups confectioner's sugar
- 1 tablespoon freshly grated lemon zest
- 2 tablespoons freshly squeezed lemon juice
- 1½ cups all-purpose flour
- ¼ cup cornstarch
- ¼ teaspoons salt

||||||||||||||||||||||||||||||||||||||||||||||||||||||||||||||||||||||||||||||

Instructions:

1. Cream the butter using an electric mixer.

2. Beat in ½ a cup of the confectioner's sugar until fluffy.

3. Mix in the fresh lemon zest and juice, followed by the flour, cornstarch, and salt. Mix until the dry ingredients are just incorporated.

4. Cover the dough with plastic wrap and chill for 60 minutes.

5. Preheat the main oven to 350 degrees F. Line 2 cookie sheets with parchment.

6. Drop spoonfuls of the dough onto the cookie sheets, 2" apart using a 1" scoop.

7. Place in the oven and bake for 12-15 minutes. Allow to cool for 5-7 minutes.

8. Add the remaining confectioner's sugar to a bowl. Toss the warm cookies in the sugar to coat.

9. Allow to cool completely before enjoying.

(4)   Apricot and Orange Liqueur Parcels

Flaky puff pastry parcels conceal a dreamy apricot filling spiked with orange liqueur.

Makes: 18

Preparation Time: 55mins

Ingredient List:

- 3 cups dried apricots (finely chopped)
- 3 teaspoons orange liqueur
- ¾ cup freshly squeezed orange juice
- ½ teaspoons cinnamon
- 3 teaspoons brown sugar

- 3 sheets ready-made puff pastry
- ½ cup whole milk
- 3 teaspoons granulated sugar

||||||||||||||||||||||||||||||||||||||||||||||||||||||||||||||||||||||||||||||

Instructions:

1. Preheat the main oven to 400 degrees F.

2. In a small saucepan over low heat, add the apricots, liqueur, juice cinnamon and brown sugar. Simmer for 5-6 minutes. Take off the heat and set to one side.

3. Slice each sheet of puff pastry into six equally sized squares.

4. In a bowl, whisk together the milk and granulated sugar.

5. Spoon filling onto 1 half of each square. Fold the empty half over the filling and seal.

6. Place the pies on a cookie sheet and brush each one generously with the milk mixture.

7. Place in the oven and bake for 12-15 minutes.

8. Serve warm.

(5) Phyllo Cups with Cappuccino Cream

Crunchy phyllo pastry makes the perfect shell to hold rich and fluffy cappuccino cream.

Makes: 12

Preparation Time: 35mins

Ingredient List:

- 6 sheets refrigerated phyllo dough (divided)

- 4 tablespoons unsalted butter (melted, divided)
- 4 tablespoons sugar (divided)
- 2 tablespoons espresso powder
- 2 cups heavy cream (chilled)
- 4 tablespoons sweetened condensed milk
- ½ teaspoons ground cinnamon
- Sea salt
- 1 teaspoon unsweetened cocoa powder

||||||||||||||||||||||||||||||||||||||||||||||||||||||||||||||||||||||

Instructions:

1. Preheat the main oven to 325 degrees F.

2. Lay two sheets of phyllo dough on a clean work surface, covering the remaining 4 phyllo dough sheets with a just-damp clean tea towel.

3. Brush the dough with ⅓ of the butter and evenly sprinkle it with 1/3 of the sugar.

4. Repeat the layering process another two times with the remaining dough, butter, and sugar.

5. Cut the stacked layers of phyllo evenly, into 6 portions, gently pressing each square into the cup of a regular sized muffin pan, and with a fork, crimping the edges as necessary in order than the phyllo is flat in the bottom of each cup.

6. Bake in the preheated oven until the phyllo is golden, approximately 20 minutes while rotating the pan 10 minutes into the cooking process. Allow to completely cool in the muffin pan on a wire baking rack.

7. In the meantime, in a medium-sized mixing bowl, combine the espresso powder along with a modest amount of heavy cream, condensed milk, ground cinnamon and a dash of salt.

8. Whisk well, until firm but not dry.

9. Transfer to the refrigerator for up to 48 hours, or until you are ready to serve.

10. When ready to serve, fill each of the phyllo cups with the cappuccino cream and scatter cocoa powder over the top

(6) Avocado Key Lime Tartlets

Although the avocado does not give an intense flavor but gives a fresh creamy texture to the tart filling that pairs perfectly with the fresh, zesty lime.

Makes: 12

Preparation Time: 3hours 30mins

Ingredient List:

- 1 cup graham crackers (crumbed)
- 2 tablespoons white sugar
- 4 tablespoons unsalted butter (melted)
- 2 small ripe avocados (pitted, peeled)
- 6 tablespoons freshly squeezed lime juice
- ½ cup sweetened condensed milk

- Slices fresh lime (for decorating)

||||||||||||||||||||||||||||||||||||||||||||||||||||||||||||||||||||||||||||

Instructions:

1. Add the crumbed crackers, sugar and butter into a food processor and pulse until combined.

2. Press 2 tablespoons of the mixture into the base of sides of each well of 2 (6-hole) mini pie pans. Pop in the freezer for 20 minutes.

3. In the meantime, add the avocado, lime juice, and condensed milk into a food processor, blitz until smooth.

4. Spoon the mixture into the frozen pie crusts.

5. Cover the pie pans with plastic kitchen wrap and chill for 2-3 hours.

6. Remove the tartlets from the pans and garnish each with a slice of lime.

(7) Pear Chips with Cinnamon Sugar

Swap out the potato chips for these oven-roasted pear chips. They are perfect served alongside dips or cheese.

Makes: 14-16 portions

Preparation Time: 3hours 10mins

Ingredient List:

- 1 cup puffed rice cereal
- 3 cups milk choc chips
- 1½ teaspoons shortening

||||||||||||||||||||||||||||||||||||||||||||||||||||||||||||||||||||||||

Instructions:

1. Cover two cookie sheets with wax paper and lightly grease. Set to one side.

2. Add the caramel and water in a heavy saucepan and gently melt over a low heat.

3. Stir in the chopped nuts and puffed rice until well covered in the caramel.

4. Take a teaspoon and scoop the mixture out into small balls and set on the cookie sheets.

5. Chill for 10-12 minutes.

6. In a clean saucepan, melt together the chocolate and shortening on a low heat.

7. Use a fork to dip the chilled caramel bites in the melted chocolate. Return to the cookie sheets and chill for 2-3 hours until set.

(9)   Orange Dreamsicle Crispy Squares

Crispy and chewy puffed rice squares are topping with a delightful peach colored topping made with natural orange flavoring.

Makes: 32

Preparation Time: 1hour 30mins

Ingredient List:

Crispy treats:

- Butter (for greasing)
- ¼ cup salted butter
- 10 ounces mini mallows
- 1½ teaspoons vanilla essence
- ½ cup boxed orange cake mix
- 6 cups puffed rice cereal
- 12 ounces white choc chips

Topping:

- 3 cups confectioner's sugar
- 6 tablespoons salted butter (room temperature)
- 6 tablespoons freshly squeezed orange juice
- ¼ teaspoons vanilla essence
- ¼ teaspoons orange essence
- Peach food gel

||||||||||||||||||||||||||||||||||||||||||||||||||||||||||||||||||||||||

Instructions:

1. Grease a rectangular pan, set aside.

2. First, make the crispy squares; in a Dutch oven over moderate-low heat, melt the butter. Add in the mini mallows and cook, while stirring, until they melt.

3. Take the mixture off the heat and stir in the vanilla essence, then the boxed cake mix.

4. Fold in the puffed rice cereal and choc chips until well incorporated and coated in the mallow mixture.

5. Gently press the mixture into the pan and allow to cool for half an hour.

6. In the meantime, prepare the topping. Beat together the sugar, butter, juice, vanilla essence, orange essence until smooth.

7. Add a few drops of the peach food coloring until you reach your desired shade.

8. Spread the orange flavored topping in a smooth even layer over the cooled mixture in the pan.

9. Put to one side until the topping sets (approximately 60 minutes), before slicing.

(10)   Caramelized Pineapple Skewers with Coconut Rum Chocolate Dipping Sauce

A coconut rum-spiked chocolate sauce is the perfect dip for tropical sweet pineapple caramelized in brown sugar.

Makes: 14-16

Preparation Time: 13mins

Ingredient List:

Sauce:

- 16 ounces 70% cocoa bittersweet chocolate (chopped)
- 1 cup coconut rum

- 1 cup whipping cream

Skewers:

- 2 ripe medium pineapples (peeled. cored, cut into small wedges)
- 1 cup dark brown sugar
- Wooden skewers

||||||||||||||||||||||||||||||||||||||||||||||||||||||||||||||||||||||

Instructions:

1. Preheat your oven's broiler.

2. Melt together the chocolate and rum using a double boiler. Take off the heat, pour in the whipping cream and stir well. Pour into one large serving bowl for dipping, or individual small cups. Set aside.

3. Thread an equal number of pineapple wedges onto each of 14-16 skewers. Arrange the skewers on a cookie sheet lined with foil.

4. Sprinkle brown sugar liberally over each skewer.

5. Place under the broiler for 2-3 minutes, until the sugar caramelizes and the pineapple becomes a little scorched at the edges.

6. Transfer to a serving plate along with the chocolate sauce.

(11) Ooey Gooey Banana Bars with Cream Cheese Frosting

Moist, gooey bars bursting with big banana flavor, all slathered with a generous layer of cream cheese bars. Guests will be begging for the recipe!

Makes: 40-42

Preparation Time: 1hour 20mins

Ingredient List:

Bars:

- 1½ cups granulated sugar
- ½ cup salted butter (room temperature)
- 1 cup sour cream
- 2 eggs
- 1 teaspoon vanilla essence
- 2 cups all-purpose flour
- ¼ teaspoons sea salt
- 1 teaspoon bicarb of soda
- 2 overripe medium bananas (pureed)

Frosting:

- ½ cup salted butter (room temperature)
- 8 ounces full-fat cream cheese
- 2 teaspoons vanilla essence
- 3½-4 cups powdered sugar

||||||||||||||||||||||||||||||||||||||||||||||||||||||||||||||||||||||||||||

Instructions:

1. Preheat the main oven to 350 degrees F.

2. Cream together the sugar and butter, until fluffy and light.

3. Beat in the sour cream, eggs, and vanilla.

4. Sift the flour, salt, and bicarb of soda into the mixture. Mix until combined.

5. Finally, fold in the banana until incorporated.

6. Place in the oven and bake for just over 20 minutes. Set aside to cool.

7. In the meantime, prepare the frosting. Beat together the butter cream cheese, and vanilla until fluffy. Beat in the powdered sugar a little at a time until you reach your preferred consistency.

8. Spread the frosting over the banana bars and serve.

(12)   Caribbean Cocktail Cupcakes

Packed with coconut, banana, and pineapple these little bites of heaven have all the flavor of your favorite holiday cocktail.

Makes: 24

Preparation Time: 1hours

Ingredient List:

Sponge:

- 2 cups granulated sugar
- 1 cup salted butter (room temperature)
- 3 medium eggs
- 2 teaspoons vanilla essence
- 2 cups mashed banana
- ½ cupped crushed pineapple
- 3 cups of all-purpose flour
- 1 teaspoon cinnamon

- 1 teaspoon bicarb of soda
- ½ teaspoons sea salt
- 1 cup walnuts (chopped)
- 1 cup coconut flakes

Frosting:

- ½ cup salted butter (at room temperature)
- 8 ounces full-fat cream cheese (at room temperature)
- 3¾ cup powdered sugar
- 1 teaspoon vanilla essence

Instructions:

1. Preheat the main oven to 350 degrees F. Fill 2 cupcake trays with liners.

2. Cream together the butter and sugar until fluffy.

3. Beat the eggs in one at a time until incorporated before stirring in the vanilla.

4. In a separate bowl, mix together the mashed banana and crushed pineapple, set aside for a moment.

5. In another clean bowl, sift together the flour, cinnamon, bicarb of soda, and salt.

6. Mix the flour mixture to the egg mixture in batches, alternating with spoonfuls of the banana/pineapple mixture.

7. Fold in the walnuts and coconut until well distributed.

8. Spoon the cupcake batter, into the cupcake trays, filling each liner ⅔ full.

9. Place in the oven and bake for 22-24 minutes. Allow to cool completely before frosting.

10. To make the frosting; beat together the butter and cream cheese, until fluffy.

11. Beat in the powdered sugar a little a time and then add the vanilla. Whisk until fluffy.

12. Pipe the frosting onto the cooled cupcakes and serve.

(13) Mocha Mousse Pots

These fluffy and creamy little mousse pots are a winning combination of dark espresso and rich chocolate flavors.

Makes: 12

Preparation Time: 8hours 10mins

Ingredient List:

- 1⅓ cups whole milk
- 12 ounces semisweet choc chips
- ½ cup egg substitute

- ¼ cup freshly brewed strong espresso
- 2 tablespoons granulated sugar
- Pinch sea salt
- Sweetened whip cream (for topping)

||||||||||||||||||||||||||||||||||||||||||||||||||||||||||||||||||||||||

Instructions:

1. Steam the milk in a heavy-bottomed saucepan for 2-3 minutes over moderate-high heat. When bubbling at the edges, take off the heat. Set aside.

2. Add the choc chips, egg substitute, espresso, sugar and, salt in a blender. Blitz until completely smooth.

3. Leave the blender running and slowly pour in the milk. Blitz for 60 seconds, until smooth.

4. Spoon the mousse into small serving glasses and chill for 6-8 hours.

5. When ready to serve, top each with a dollop of whip cream.

(14)   Coffee Ice Cream Stuffed Profiteroles

These homemade profiteroles are surprisingly easy to make and will definitely impress family and friends with their coffee ice cream center and hot fudge topping.

Makes: 24

Preparation Time: 1hour 30mins

Ingredient List:

- 1½ teaspoons granulated sugar
- ¾ cup all-purpose flour

- ⅓ cup salted butter
- ¾ cup water
- 3 eggs (lightly beaten)
- 1½ cups coffee flavor ice cream
- Hot fudge ice cream topping (for serving)

||||||||||||||||||||||||||||||||||||||||||||||||||||||||||||||||||||||||

Instructions:

1. Preheat the main oven to 400 degrees F; line a baking sheet with parchment paper.

2. Sift together the sugar and flour into a bowl. Set aside.

3. In a large saucepan, bring to boil the butter and water, while stirring. Take off the heat.

4. Immediately mix the butter mixture with the flour mixture and using a wooden spoon beat* until the batter pulls away from the sides of the pan to form a smooth ball of dough.

5. One at a time, beat in the eggs until the mixture is glossy.

6. Take a tablespoon and drop rounds of dough onto the baking sheet.

7. Place in the oven and bake until golden and puffy, approximately 20 minutes.

8. Make a steam hole in each profiterole using a sharp knife and set aside to cool completely.

9. Slice each profiterole in half and spoon a little coffee ice cream onto the bottom halves. Replace the tops of the profiteroles and refrigerate until ready to serve.

10. Arrange on a serving platter and drizzle with plenty of hot fudge sauce,

*Preferably using a wooden spoon.

(15) Mini Vanilla Baked Cheesecakes

Creamy and tangy, with a vanilla wafer base, these scrumptious mini cheesecakes can be made with the minimum of fuss.

Makes: 16

Preparation Time: 25mins

Ingredient List:

- 16 vanilla wafers
- ¾ cup granulated sugar
- 16 ounces full-fat cream cheese (room temperature)
- 2 medium eggs
- 1 teaspoon vanilla essence

IIIIIIIIIIIIIIIIIIIIIIIIIIIIIIIIIIIIIIIIIIIIIIIIIIIIIIIIIIIIIIIIIIIIIIII

Instructions:

1. Preheat the main oven to 350 degrees F. Fill 2 (8 hole) cupcake tins with liners.

2. Place a vanilla wafer in the base of each liner.

3. Beat together the sugar and cream cheese until smooth.

4. Beat in the eggs and vanilla essence until combined.

5. Spoon the cheesecake mixture into the liners.

6. Bake in the oven until set, approximately 15 minutes.

7. Serve at room temperature.

(16)   Custard Pear Bars with Macadamia Nuts

These divine bars are a real party pleaser thanks to the macadamia nut sponge base, creamy custard middle, and cinnamon spiced pear topping.

Makes: 16

Preparation Time: 4hours 15mins

Ingredient List:

Base:

- ⅓ cup granulated sugar
- ½ cup salted butter (room temperature)
- ¼ teaspoons vanilla essence
- ¾ cup all-purpose flour
- ⅔ cup raw macadamia nuts (finely chopped)

Custard:

- ½ cup granulated sugar
- 8 ounces full-fat cream cheese (room temperature)
- ½ teaspoons vanilla essence
- 1 egg
- Pear topping:
- 1 (15¼ ounce) can pear halves (drained, sliced ⅛" thick, blotted dry)
- 1 teaspoon cinnamon sugar

IIIIIIIIIIIIIIIIIIIIIIIIIIIIIIIIIIIIIIIIIIIIIIIIIIIIIIIIIIIIIIIIIIIIIIIIIII

Instructions:

1. Preheat the main oven to 350 degrees F. Grease a square baking dish and set to one side.

2. Cream together the sugar and butter until fluffy. Stir in the vanilla essence.

3. Beat in the flour a little at a time until incorporated and then fold in the nuts.

4. Press the mixture into the baking dish. Place in the oven and bake for 18-20 minutes. Take out of the oven and set aside to cool. Turn the oven up to 375 degrees F.

5. Beat together the sugar and cream cheese until fluffy. Stir in the vanilla essence.

6. Beat in the egg until just incorporated.

7. Spread the mixture over the cooled crust.

8. Place the sliced pears on top of the custard in a single layer and sprinkle over the cinnamon sugar.

9. Return to the oven and bake for just under half an hour.

10. Allow to cool completely at room temperature before transferring to the refrigerator for 2-3 hours.

11. Slice and serve at room temperature.

(17)   Mini Sugar Cookie Pizzas

Kids and grownups will go crazy for these adorable and yummy mini pizzas with their buttery sugar cookie base, cheesecake spread, and fruity toppings.

Makes: 40

Preparation Time: 45mins

Ingredient List:

Cookies:

- ½ cup shortening
- ½ cup salted butter
- 2 teaspoons baking powder
- 2 cups granulated sugar
- Pinch sea salt
- ½ teaspoons vanilla essence
- Yolks from 3 medium eggs
- 2½ cups all-purpose flour

Cheesecake spread:

- ½ cup confectioner's sugar
- 8 ounces full-fat cream cheese (at room temperature)
- 1 cup heavy cream
- Fresh fruit (cut into bite-sized pieces)

||||||||||||||||||||||||||||||||||||||||||||||||||||||||||||||||||

Instructions:

1. Preheat the main oven to 300 degrees F.

2. Beat together the shortening and butter. Mix in the baking powder, sugar, and salt.

3. Finally, add the vanilla and egg yolks, and then fold through the flour until incorporated.

4. Roll dough, using hands, into 1" balls and set on a cookie sheet.

5. Place in the oven and bake for 10-12 minutes.

6. Allow to cool on the cookie sheet before turning the oven off and setting aside to cool completely.

7. In the meantime, prepare the spread. Beat together the confectioner's sugar and cream cheese until smooth.

8. While still mixing, pour in the cream and whisk until the mixture becomes thick.

9. Spread a layer of the cheesecake mixture onto each cooled cookie and top each with fresh fruit.

10. Enjoy!

(18)   Fried Apple Pies

Spiced apple pie filling sits inside deep-fried pockets of crispy golden pastry.

Makes: 24

Preparation Time: 35mins

Ingredient List:

- 8 ounces dried apple (soaked overnight, drained, rinsed)
- 1 cup water
- 2 tablespoons salted butter (melted)
- ¼ teaspoons nutmeg
- 1 teaspoon cinnamon
- ¾ cup granulated sugar

- 2 tablespoons freshly squeezed lemon juice
- Prepared pastry for 1 (10") pie
- Canola oil

||||||||||||||||||||||||||||||||||||||||||||||||||||||||||||||||||||||||

Instructions:

1. In a large saucepan add the apple and water, heat until boiling. Turn the heat down low, cover and cook gently for half an hour, until tender. Drain and set aside to cool.

2. Stir the butter, nutmeg, cinnamon, sugar, and lemon juice into the apples. Use a potato masher to squash the mixture into a thick puree. Set to one side for a moment.

3. Divide the dough into three equal portions and then roll each portion into a ⅛" sheet. Cut 4" circles out of the pastry.

4. Spoon 1 tablespoon of apple puree into one half of each circle of pastry. Use damp fingers to wet the edges of the pastry. Fold the unfilled half of pastry over the filling and seal the seams using a flour-dipped fork.

5. Pour an inch of oil into a large skillet and heat to 375 degrees F.

6. Fry the pastries until browned and golden on each side.

7. Pat off excess oil with kitchen paper and serve warm.

(19) Little Monster's Fruitsicles

Just one ingredient is all you need to make these tropical fruitsicles that your little monsters will love.

Makes: 14-16

Preparation Time: 8hours 5mins

Ingredient List:

- 2 cans (20 ounces each) tropical fruit cocktail with juice

||||||||||||||||||||||||||||||||||||||||||||||||||||||||||||||||||||||||

Instructions:

1. Spoon the fruit cocktail and a little juice into two (8 hole) popsicle molds with handles.

2. Freeze for 7-8 hours until set. If you have trouble removing the popsicles from the molds, run the cups under a little warm water to help loosen them.

(20) Italian Christmas Cookies

Adding ricotta to the cookie dough makes an extra moist Christmas cookie. Be sure to make plenty; these cookies will disappear quickly!

Makes: 100

Preparation Time: 40mins

Ingredient List:

Cookies:

- Butter (for greasing)
- 2 cups granulated sugar
- 1 cup salted butter (softened)
- 3 eggs
- 2 teaspoons vanilla essence
- 15 ounces ricotta cheese
- 4 cups all-purpose flour
- 1 teaspoon sea salt

- 1 teaspoon bicarb of soda

Frosting:

- 3-4 cups powdered sugar
- ¼ cup salted butter (softened)
- ½ teaspoons vanilla essence
- 3-4 tablespoons whole milk
- Sprinkles

||||||||||||||||||||||||||||||||||||||||||||||||||||||||||||||||||||||||||||

Instructions:

1. Preheat the main oven to 350 degrees F. Grease two cookie sheets.

2. Cream together the sugar and butter.

3. One at a time, beat in the eggs until incorporated, followed by the vanilla essence and ricotta.

4. In a clean bowl, sift together the flour, salt, and bicarb of soda. Add the flour mixture to the egg mixture in batches, mixing until incorporated.

5. Drop teaspoons of the cookie dough onto the cookie sheets.

6. Place in the oven and bake for just over 10 minutes. Allow to cool totally before frosting.

7. To make the frosting; beat together the powdered sugar, butter, vanilla and just enough to milk to make a spreadable frosting.

8. Spread the frosting on top of the cooled cookies and scatter over sprinkles.

9. Keep chilled.

Chapter II: Savory Recipes

||||||||||||||||||||||||||||||||||||||||||||||||||||||||||||||||||||||||||||||

(21)   Upside-Down Mushroom Tartlets

These veggie tartlets are a quick and easy finger food ideal for a festive get-together.

Servings: 12

Preparation Time: 1hour

Ingredient List:

- 2 sheets frozen pastry (thawed, cut into 6 (3") rounds)
- 2 tablespoons virgin olive oil
- 2 large shallots (diced small)
- 2-pound Cremini mushrooms (sliced)
- Sea salt and black pepper
- 4 teaspoons fresh thyme leaves

- 1½ cups Gruyere cheese (grated)
- Thyme (to garnish)

||||||||||||||||||||||||||||||||||||||||||||||||||||||||||||||||||||||||

Instructions:

1. Preheat the main oven to 375 degrees F.

2. Arrange the pastry rounds in one single layer on a baking sheet lined with parchment paper and place in the refrigerator while you are cooking the mushrooms.

3. In a large frying pan or skillet over moderate heat, heat the oil.

4. Add the shallots and cook, while stirring, until softened, 2-3 minutes.

5. Add the sliced mushrooms and cook, while stirring until browned and softened, 8-10 minutes and season with salt and black pepper. Add the thyme and stir. Take the pan off the heat.

6. Lightly grease 12 jumbo muffin cups. Evenly divide the mixture along with the grated cheese between the 12 cups, and top with a chilled round of pastry.

7. Bake in the oven until the pastry is puffed and golden, about 25 minutes, rotating the pan halfway through the baking process.

8. Run a small, sharp knife around each cup to loosen the tartlets.

9. To release the tartlets, place a baking sheet over the pan and invert.

10. Sprinkle with additional thyme and serve warm.

(22)   Antipasti Pizzas

Add Italian flair and flavor with these delicious pizza nibbles.

Makes: 32

Preparation Time: 20mins

Ingredient List:

- 2 tablespoons extra virgin oil
- 1-pound chilled pizza dough
- Sea salt and black pepper
- 1 cup mozzarella (shredded)
- ½ cup artichoke hearts (thinly sliced)
- ½ cup olives (pitted, coarsely chopped)
- 1 teaspoon red pepper flakes (to garnish)

||||||||||||||||||||||||||||||||||||||||||||||||||||||||||||||||||

Instructions:

1. Preheat the main oven to 450 degrees F.

2. Grease two baking sheets with olive oil.

3. Evenly divide the dough into 32 equal-sized portions.

4. Flour your work surface, and using the palm of your hand gently press each portion into a 2" round shape.

5. Transfer the rounds to the baking sheets, flipping them over once to lightly coat in olive oil.

6. Season with sea salt and black pepper.

7. Divide the shredded mozzarella, artichokes, and olives between the 32 rounds.

8. Sprinkle with pepper flakes.

9. Bake in the preheated oven for 10-12 minutes or until the cheese bubbles and the dough is golden.

(23)   Sun-Dried Tomato Palmiers

Elegant palmiers made from puff and filled with sun-dried tomatoes are go-to hor 'd oeuvres.

Makes: 12

Preparation Time: 25mins

Ingredient List:

- 2 sheets frozen puff pastry (thawed)
- 6 tablespoons ricotta cheese
- 6 tablespoons sun-dried tomato paste (divided)
- 4 ounces Parmesan cheese (grated)

||||||||||||||||||||||||||||||||||||||||||||||||||||||||||||||||||||||

Instructions:

1. Preheat the main oven to 425 degrees F.

2. Roll out one sheet of puff pastry into a rectangular shape of around 1/8"thick and trim to approximately 8x11".

3. Spread three tablespoons of ricotta cheese onto the pastry.

4. Spread three tablespoons of tomato paste on top.

5. Sprinkle half of the Parmesan on top.

6. Reach the long side of the pastry into the middle of the rectangle, making sure the pastry is even and tight.

7. Repeat the process with the other sheet of puff pastry, remaining ricotta cheese, tomato paste, and grated Parmesan.

8. Individually wrap each roll in a plastic wrap and place in the fridge until firm, for around half an hour.

9. Take the rolls out of the refrigerator and slice into ½" thick slices.

10. Place the palmiers around 2-3" apart on a baking sheet lined with a parchment paper.

11. Bake in the oven until golden and puffy, 7-9 minutes.

12. Turn the palmiers over and bake until golden.

13. Allow to completely cool on a wire baking rack.

(24) Balsamic, Fruit and Cheese Bruschetta

A French baguette is topped with creamy goat cheese and a mixture of strawberries, nectarine, tomatoes and balsamic vinegar to create the tastiest party nibble.

Makes: 10

Preparation Time: 35mins

Ingredient List:

- 1½ cups fresh strawberries (sliced)
- 1 nectarine (diced)
- 1 cup grape tomatoes (quartered)
- 3 tablespoons fresh basil (thinly sliced)
- 1 shallot (minced)
- 2 tablespoons olive oil
- 1 tablespoon balsamic vinegar
- 1 teaspoon sugar
- 1 teaspoon freshly ground pepper
- ¼ teaspoons salt
- 1 (12 ounce) French bread baguette
- 1 (10 ounce) goat cheese log (softened)

||||||||||||||||||||||||||||||||||||||||||||||||||||||||||||||||||||||

Instructions:

1. Preheat the main oven to 375 degrees F.

2. In a mixing bowl, combine the strawberries with the nectarine, tomatoes, basil, shallot, olive oil, vinegar, sugar, freshly ground pepper and salt. Stir well.

3. Cut the baguette in half, cutting each half crosswise into 4 equal pieces.

4. Spread the cut sides of the baguette slices with goat cheese.

5. Place the slices of bread on a baking tray and bake for 12-15 minutes, or until heated through.

6. Remove from the oven and top with the strawberry mixture. Cut into slices of approximately 2" thick and serve.

(25)   Spanish Chorizo Skewers

Smoky and flavorsome chorizo skewers are a welcome change to the classic party foods.

Makes: 24

Preparation Time: 8hours 45mins

Ingredient List:

- 7 ounces waxy potatoes (peeled, cut into 24 (1") cubes)
- 1 tablespoon sunflower oil
- 2 teaspoons fresh rosemary (finely chopped)
- Salt and pepper
- 1 red pepper (seeded, cut into 24 (1") chunks)
- 1 yellow pepper (seeded, cut into 24 (1") chunks)
- 7 ounces cooking chorizo (cut into 24 pieces)

Garlic dip:

- 7 ounces half-fat crème fraiche
- 1 clove garlic (crushed)
- ½ small pack flat-leaf parsley (finely chopped)

||||||||||||||||||||||||||||||||||||||||||||||||||||||||||||||||||||||||||||

Instructions:

1. Preheat the main oven to 400 degrees F. Fill a large pot or pan to half capacity with water and bring to boil.

2. Add the cubes of potatoes, and return to the boil. Cook for 60 seconds, and then using a colander drain, and tip into a mixing bowl.

3. Pour over the sunflower oil, and scatter with rosemary, seasoning well with salt and pepper and toss to combine.

4. Arrange the cubes of potatoes on a large baking sheet and cook for 5 minutes, turning the potatoes, add the red and yellow peppers and cook for a further 8-10 minutes, or until beginning to soften. Set to one side to cool.

5. Thread a chunk of red pepper, a cube of potato and a chunk of yellow pepper onto wooden skewers; finish off with a chunk of chorizo.

6. Arrange the skewers on a baking tray lined with parchment paper, cover, and chill, for up to 8 hours.

7. Next, make the dip: In a mixing bowl, combine the crème fraiche, garlic, and parsley, cover and transfer to the fridge to chill.

8. When you are ready to serve, heat in the preheated oven for 10 minutes, or until the veggies are beginning to soften and brown and the slices of chorizo are cooked and heated through.

9. Serve with the garlic dip.

(26)   Blini with Caviar

Traditional Russian pancakes will make sure your party dazzles.

Makes: 48

Preparation Time: 2hours

Ingredient List:

- 2¼ teaspoons active dry yeast
- ½ cup warm water (110 degrees)
- 1 cup all-purpose flour
- Sea salt
- ½ cup low-fat buttermilk

- 1 tablespoon unsalted butter (melted)
- ½ teaspoons sugar
- 2 large eggs (separated)
- Butter (to grease)
- Crème fraiche (to garnish)
- Trout roe (to garnish)
- Salmon (to garnish)

||||||||||||||||||||||||||||||||||||||||||||||||||||||||||||||||||||||

Instructions:

1. In a small bowl, sprinkle the dry yeast over the warm water. Allow to stand for 4-5 minutes, or until foamy.

2. In a mixing bowl, combine the flour with ½ teaspoon of sea salt plus an additional pinch; stir to incorporate.

3. In a large bowl, stir the buttermilk, together with the melted butter, sugar and two egg yolks, whisk in the yeast mixture followed by the flour-salt mixture. Allow to rest, covered with a clean tea towel, at room temperature for half an hour.

4. In a bowl, beat the two egg whites until stiff peaks begin to form, and fold into the batter. Allow to rest for 10 minutes.

5. Set a medium-sized frying pan or skillet over moderate heat, and coat with a fine layer of butter.

6. Add a small amount of batter to make each blini, and working in batches of 5 to 6 per pan, cook, flip each blini over when the edges begin to bubble, and the batter becomes golden, this will take around ½ -2minutes each side.

7. Transfer to a baking tray, lined with parchment paper and allow to cool for 30-40 minutes.

8. Garnish each blini with crème fraiche.

9. Top half of your blini with trout roe and the other half with salmon.

(27) Smoked Salmon and Caramelized Onion Stuffed Celery Stalks

Crunchy and crisp celery stuffed with onions and garnished with smoked salmon.

Makes: 12

Preparation Time: 50mins

Ingredient List:

- 1 tablespoon olive oil
- 1 red onion (sliced thinly)
- 2 teaspoons granulated sugar
- 8 ounces full-fat cream cheese (whipped)

- 5 tablespoons white horseradish (squeezed)
- 5 ounces smoked salmon
- 9 sticks celery (strings removed, chopped into 2" pieces)
- Small tips of dill (to garnish)

||||||||||||||||||||||||||||||||||||||||||||||||||||||||||||||||||||

Instructions:

1. In a frying pan, heat the olive oil over moderate heat. Add the slices of onion and turn the heat down low. Cook, occasionally stirring for approximately 15 minutes.

2. Add the sugar and cook while stirring until the onions begin to caramelize, for approximately half an hour.

3. Take off the heat and set to one side.

4. In a medium-sized mixing bowl combine the cream cheese along with the horseradish. Evenly divide the mixture between 2 bowls.

5. Coarsely chop ¼ of the salmon and add to ½ of the cheese mixture, add the dill and stir to combine.

6. Slice the remaining smoked salmon into fine slivers and set to one side.

7. Fill half of the celery with the mixture.

8. Garnish each piece with a salmon sliver and garnish with one or two dill tips.

9. Fill the remaining celery with the leftover cheese mixture, and garnish with caramelized onions.

10. Serve.

(28) Chicken Liver Pate Crostini with Quince Jelly

Quince jelly pairs with chicken liver pate to make perfect festive finger food.

Makes: 48

Preparation Time: 2hours 30mins

Ingredient List:

- 1½ sticks unsalted butter (room temperature, divided)
- 3 shallots (finely chopped)
- 1 tablespoon garlic (minced)
- 1-pound chicken livers (rinsed, trimmed)

- Coarse salt
- ⅛ teaspoons cayenne pepper
- ½ cup dry white wine
- 1 teaspoon fresh thyme
- Black pepper
- 1 French baguette (sliced lengthwise into ¼ "thick rounds)
- Virgin olive oil (for brushing)
- Quince jelly (to serve)

||||||||||||||||||||||||||||||||||||||||||||||||||||||||||||||||||||||||

Instructions:

1. Line a 4x6" loaf pan with plastic wrap.

2. Melt two tablespoons of the butter in a large skillet over moderate to high heat, until foamy.

3. Add the shallots and garlic to the pan and cook for 2 minutes, or until softened.

4. Next, add the chicken livers along with one teaspoon of salt, and the cayenne pepper, and cook while occasionally stirring for 10 minutes.

5. Take the pan off the heat and add the white wine and fresh thyme.

6. Return to the heat, cover and cook for 5-6 minutes, or until the liquid reduces by 50%.

7. In a food processor, pulse the chicken livers together with the pan juices and remaining butter, until silky smooth. Season with salt and black pepper.

8. Pour the mixture into a pan and using a spatula, smooth over. Transfer the pan to the fridge to set, for around 2 hours.

9. Preheat the main oven to 375 degrees F.

10. Lightly brush the slices of baguette with olive oil and toast.

11. Sprinkle each slice with sea salt.

12. Remove the chicken liver pate from the pan and spread onto the toast.

13. Spoon a little quince jelly over the plate.

(29) Scallop Horseradish Finger Food

An incredible amuse bouche.

Makes: 20

Preparation Time: 4mins

Ingredient List:

- 20 medium fresh scallops
- Butter (to fry)

- Cayenne pepper (to garnish)
- Beet horseradish spread (readymade)
- 1 English cucumber (cut into 20 ¼" slices)
- Sea salt
- 1 scallion (finely chopped)

‖‖

Instructions:

1. Using kitchen paper towel, pat the scallops dry.

2. In a frying pan, heat a dab of butter, when hot and melted, quickly sear the scallops for 2-3 minutes, taking care not to overcook. Add a dash of cayenne pepper.

3. Spread a little horseradish spread on top of each slice of cucumber and then placed a cooked scallop on top.

4. Sprinkle with sea salt and finely chopped scallions.

(30)   Cocktail Mini Meatballs

Melt in the mouth mini meatballs are always a party pleaser.

Makes: 48

Preparation Time: 1hour 30mins

Ingredient List:

- 2 slices soft white bread (torn into bite-size pieces)
- ½ cup whole milk
- 1-pound ground pork
- 1-pound ground beef chuck
- 6 thin slices pancetta (finely diced)
- ½ small onion (minced)
- 2 large egg yolks (lightly beaten)
- Sea salt and freshly ground pepper
- ½ teaspoons mild smoked paprika
- 2 teaspoons fresh thyme (finely chopped)
- Extra-virgin olive oil (for frying)

||||||||||||||||||||||||||||||||||||||||||||||||||||||||||||||||||

Instructions:

1. Soak the bread in the milk in a large mixing bowl. Add the pork, beef, pancetta, and minced onion and using clean hands mix to combine. Add the two large, lightly beaten egg yolks along with 2 teaspoons sea salt, a dash of black pepper, paprika, and thyme.

2. Using clean hands form the mixture into 48 evenly sized balls, of around 1-1 ¼".

3. Chill the mini meatballs, in a single layer for 60 minutes.

4. Preheat the main oven to 300 degrees F. Lightly coat a large frying pan or skillet with olive oil and fry, in batches if necessary, the meatballs in a single layer over moderate to high heat for 7-8 minutes, or until browned on all sides.

5. Repeat the process until all of the meatballs are cooked.

6. Transfer the meatballs to a baking sheet and cook for 10-15 minutes, until cooked through.

(31) Sausage-Cheddar Balls

Sausage, cheese, and onion combine to make a flavorsome finger food for hungry guests.

Makes: 45

Preparation Time: 35mins

Ingredient List:

- 1¼ cups all-purpose flour
- ½ teaspoons coarse salt
- ¼ teaspoons ground pepper
- ½ teaspoons cayenne pepper
- 1½ teaspoons baking powder
- 2 cups Cheddar cheese (grated)
- 1-pound breakfast sausage (casings removed, crumbled)
- ½ large yellow onion, grated on large holes of a box grater

3 • tablespoons unsalted butter (melted)

||||||||||||||||||||||||||||||||||||||||||||||||||||||||||||||||||||||||||||

Instructions:

1. Preheat the main oven to 400 degrees F.

2. In a large mixing bowl, whisk the flour along with the salt and pepper, cayenne pepper and baking powder.

3. Add the grated Cheddar and toss to coat evenly.

4. Add the breakfast sausage, onion, and melted butter.

5. Using clean hands mix until incorporated and roll the mixture into 1" balls.

6. Arrange the balls, around ½ "apart on a baking sheet lined with parchment paper.

7. Bake in the oven until the balls are golden, cooked, and heated through (20-25 minutes).

8. Serve warm.

(32)   Coconut Chicken Fingers with Banana Dip

Crispy coconut chicken fingers served with a sweet and sour banana ketchup dip will make you a popular host.

Makes: 8

Preparation Time: 40mins

Ingredient List:

- 4 medium bananas (peeled)
- 6 tablespoons rice wine vinegar
- 1 jalapeño (seeded, roughly chopped)
- ½ medium onion (chopped)
- 1½ tablespoons fresh ginger (chopped)
- 1 teaspoon curry powder
- ½ teaspoons ground allspice
- 2 tablespoons soy sauce
- 1 tablespoon vanilla extract
- 3 tablespoons tomato paste

For the chicken fingers:

- 1¾ pounds chicken tenderloins (halved lengthwise)
- 1 ½ tablespoons coconut oil
- Salt and freshly ground black pepper
- 1¼ cups shredded unsweetened coconut (shredded)
- ¾ cup panko

||||||||||||||||||||||||||||||||||||||||||||||||||||||||||||||||||||

Instructions:

1. To a food blender or processor add the bananas, vinegar, jalapeno, chopped onion, ginger, curry powder, allspice, soy sauce, vanilla extract and tomato paste and blitz until silky smooth and lump free. Set the mixture to one side, until time to serve.

2. Preheat the main oven to 375 degrees F. Line a baking sheet with parchment paper.

3. Add the chicken to a large mixing bowl and drizzle with coconut oil and generously season with salt and black pepper. Mix well, until the chicken is well and evenly coated with the coconut oil.

4. Add the shredded coconut along with the panko crumbs to a ziplock bag and shake well to combine.

5. Add around half of the chicken fingers to the bag and shake to coat evenly.

6. Arrange the coated chicken fingers on a baking sheet.

7. Repeat the process until all of the fingers are coated.

8. Bake in the preheated oven for between 15-20 minutes, or until the chicken's juices run clear, and the chicken is sufficiently cooked through. Take care though, not to overcook.

9. Serve the coconut chicken fingers with banana ketchup dip.

(33) Prosciutto Crisps

Naughty nibbles to enjoy with a cheeky cocktail or two!

Makes: 12

Preparation Time: 12mins

Ingredient List:

- 12 prosciutto slices (very thinly sliced)
- 36 fresh sage leaves
- 2 tablespoons olive oil

||||||||||||||||||||||||||||||||||||||||||||||||||||||||||||||||||||||||||||||||

Instructions:

1. Toss the slices of prosciutto with the sage leaves and olive oil.

2. Arrange the slices, laid out flat, on a baking sheet lined with a parchment paper and bake at 350 degrees for 10-12 minutes, or until crisp.

3. Remove from the oven and allow to slightly cool.

4. Break the slices into pieces and serve.

(34) Curried Pea and Potato Samosas

Crunchy Samosas make for a moreish party snack.

Makes: 12

Preparation Time: 50mins

Ingredient List:

- Salt
- 14 ounces potatoes (peeled, chopped finely)
- 1 yellow onion (diced)
- 2 garlic cloves (chopped)
- 1 teaspoon ground turmeric
- 2 teaspoons cumin seeds
- 2 teaspoons ground coriander
- ¼-½ red chili (deseeded, chopped finely)

- Juice of 1 lime
- 1 cup frozen petit pois
- Black pepper
- Handful coriander leaves (roughly chopped)
- 3 sheets flaky pastry (thawed)
- 1 medium egg (lightly beaten)

Dip:

- ½ cup plain yogurt
- Handful mint leaves (roughly chopped)
- Juice of ½ a lime

||||||||||||||||||||||||||||||||||||||||||||||||||||||||||||||||||||

Instructions:

1. In a large pan of salted water, bring the potatoes to boil, cooking until fork tender.

2. Drain the potatoes and put to one side.

3. In a saucepan heat a splash of oil and add the onion along with the garlic, cooking over low to moderate heat, until the onion has softened.

4. Add the turmeric, cumin, and coriander, adding an additional splash of olive oil to the pan if needed.

5. Add the chopped chili together with the lime juice and frozen baby peas. Cover the pan with a lid and cook for 4-5 minutes, or until the peas are fork tender, regularly stirring.

6. Add the diced potato to the pea mixture along with the coriander and mix.

7. Season well with salt and black pepper and set to one side to cool.

8. Preheat the main oven to 400 degrees F.

9. Cut each sheet of pastry into four pieces and place one spoonful of filling into the center of each square.

10. Dampen the edges of the pastry and fold over to form a triangular shape and seal the edges with a metal fork.

11. Place the samosas on a baking sheet lined with parchment paper. Brush each samosa with a drop of milk or a little beaten egg.

12. Bake in the oven for 17-20 minutes, until the pastry is golden brown and the filling is hot.

13. While the samosas cool down, make the dip by mixing the yogurt, mint leaves and lime juice in a small bowl.

14. Serve the samosas with the mint and yogurt dip.

(35)   Pancetta-Wrapped Figs

When Black Mission Figs are combined with savory ingredients, they can produce a "meaty" flavor that has a smoky aroma. They are perfect paired with salty pancetta.

Makes: 36

Preparation Time: 2 hours 10mins

Ingredient List:

- ½ cup red wine vinegar
- ½ cup water
- 1 tablespoon light brown sugar
- 1 tablespoon juniper berries
- 10 whole black peppercorns
- 2 whole cloves

- 1 cup dried Black Mission figs (stemmed)
- 12 ounces pancetta (sliced into ⅛" thick rounds cut into ½" thick strips)

||||||||||||||||||||||||||||||||||||||||||||||||||||||||||||||||||||||||||

Instructions:

1. In a pan, bring the red wine vinegar, water, brown sugar, juniper berries, black peppercorns and cloves to a boil.

2. Add the figs and gently simmer for 5 minutes.

3. Take the pan off the heat, cover and set to one side to rest, until the mixture is room temperature.

4. Preheat the main oven to 350 degrees F.

5. Using a slotted kitchen utensil, arrange the figs on a chopping board and slice in half.

6. Wrap strip of pancetta around each half of fig.

7. Transfer the wrapped dates, seam side facing down, to a wire baking rack, set on a baking tray.

8. Bake in the oven until the pancetta browns, approximately 30 minutes.

9. Secure each wrapped fig with a cocktail stick.

10. Serve warm.

(36) Dates Stuffed with Blue Cheese

It's probably a good idea to double up on this recipe as tasty morsels are bound to disappear pretty quickly.

Makes: 12

Preparation Time: 22mins

Ingredient List:

- 12 dates (pitted)
- 2 ounces Gorgonzola cheese
- 1 tablespoon sliced almonds (toasted)
- Greek honey (to drizzle)

|||||||||||||||||||||||||||||||||||||||||||||||||||||||||||||||||||||||||

Instructions:

1. Use a sharp kitchen knife to cut a slit into each of the dates and stuff with Gorgonzola cheese.

2. Then arrange the stuffed dates on your serving platter and scatter with almonds.

3. Drizzle with honey and serve.

(37)   Mini Spaghetti Pies

Little fingers won't be able to resist these tiny tempting party treats.

Makes: 24

Preparation Time: 40mins

Ingredient List:

- 12 slices sandwich bread
- ¼ cup butter (melted)
- 10½ ounces canned spaghetti in tomato sauce
- ⅓ cup cheese (grated)
- 3 rashers bacon (chopped)

||||||||||||||||||||||||||||||||||||||||||||||||||||||||||||||||||||||||

Instructions:

1. First, trim the crusts from the sandwich bread and brush only one side of each bread slice with melted butter.

2. Push the slices of bread, buttered side facing down into a 12 cup muffin tin.

3. Fill each muffin cup with a spoonful of spaghetti, and top with grated cheese and bacon.

4. Bake at 350 degrees F until crispy, approximately 15 minutes, or until the cheese melts, the bacon is crispy and the filling hot.

5. Allow to cool a little before serving.

(38)   Feta, Mango and Watermelon Skewers

Salty feta, sweet mango, and juicy watermelon are a modern take on the classic cheese and pineapple cocktail party favorite.

Makes: 20

Preparation Time: 40mins

Ingredient List:

- I large mango (peeled, seeded, diced into 10 cubes)
- 14 ounces watermelon flesh (peeled, seeded, cut into 10 cubes)
- 7 ounces feta cheese (cut into 20 cubes)
- 1 teaspoon poppy seeds (toasted)

- 1 lime (optional, to serve)

||||||||||||||||||||||||||||||||||||||||||||||||||||||||||||||||||||||

Instructions:

1. Place the mango on one plate, watermelon on a second and feta cubes on a third.

2. Scatter all 3 with poppy seeds, and gently toss so the seeds adhere.

3. Make ten skewers, alternating with cubes of feta and cubes and mango and the other ten skewers with cubes of feta and cubes of watermelon.

4. Transfer all 20 to a large serving plate, squeeze lime juice over all 20 skewers and cover and chill in the fridge for 20-30 minutes before you are ready to serve.

(39) Goat Cheese, Cranberry, and Walnut Canapés

Tasty canapés add a touch of style to any get-together or party.

Makes: 24

Preparation Time: 40mins

Ingredient List:

- 24 walnut halves
- 4 teaspoons olive oil (divided)
- ⅛ teaspoons ground cinnamon
- Sea salt and black pepper

- ½ whole-wheat baguette (cut into 24 thin slices)
- 8 ounces fresh goat cheese
- ½ cup dried cranberries
- 1 teaspoon fresh thyme (chopped)
- Thyme leaves (to garnish)

‖‖

Instructions:

1. Preheat the main oven to 375 degrees F.

2. On a large rimmed baking tray or sheet, toss the walnut halves along with one teaspoon of olive oil and ground cinnamon and season with sea salt and black pepper.

3. Bake in the oven until golden, for 4-6 minutes. Set to one side to cool.

4. Arrange the slices of baguette on the same sheet and lightly brush with the remaining teaspoon of oil and season well with salt and pepper.

5. Bake in the oven for 12-15 minutes or until lightly toasted, turn the slices over, halfway through toasting. Set to one side to cool

6. In the meantime, in a medium-sized mixing bowl, stir the cheese with 2 tablespoons of water until silky smooth, add the cranberries and thyme and stir to incorporate.

7. Season with salt and black pepper.

8. Evenly divide the goat cheese between the 24 slices of toasted bread, topping each one with a walnut half and garnishing with a thyme leaf.

(40)   Fried Mozzarella

These irresistible gooey and cheesy bite-size balls make the best ever finger food treats.

Makes: 40

Preparation Time: 30mins

Ingredient List:

- 1 cup all-purpose flour
- 2 large eggs
- 1 cup panko
- 1 teaspoon dried thyme
- Sea salt and black pepper
- 1-pound bocconcini (egg size mozzarella balls)
- 2 cups vegetable oil
- Tomato sauce (to serve)

||||||||||||||||||||||||||||||||||||||||||||||||||||||||||||||||||||

Instructions:

1. Preheat the main oven to 250 degrees F.

2. To a large mixing bowl, add the flour.

3. In a second bowl, beat the eggs.

4. In a third mixing bowl, combine the panko along with the thyme.

5. Season the ingredients in each bowl with salt and black pepper.

6. Working in batches of 2, dredge the mozzarella balls (bocconcini) in flour, shaking to remove any excess, coat each ball in egg and roll in the panko-thyme mixture, press gently to ensure that the panko sticks.

7. In a saucepan over moderate to high heat, heat the oil.

8. Fry the mozzarella balls, in batches of 4, until golden; they will need to be occasionally turned.

9. Using a slotted spoon, transfer the ball to kitchen paper and season well with salt.

10. Keep the balls warm in the oven and repeat the process until all of the bocconcini are cooked.

11. Serve with a tomato dipping sauce.

Made in the USA
Las Vegas, NV
14 September 2024